Chevron

Wrap yourself in comfort and luxury with ever-popular Caron® Simply Soft®. This premium yarn has no equal for its weight, luster and sheen, and its soft drape makes it the right choice for throws and garments alike. Machine washable and dryable, Simply Soft really delivers on the details, with no-dye-lot solids and ombres, plus heathers that produce a sophisticated effect. The throws in this chevron collection are creative examples of the beautiful possibilities of Caron Simply Soft!

About Spinrite:
Established in 1952, Spinrite LP is North America's largest craft yarn producer. Its well-known brands include Patons, Bernat, Caron, and Lily Sugar 'n Cream. For more about Spinrite, visit Yarnspirations.com, a one-stop resource for everything that you need to create knit and crochet projects to suit any mood, budget, or occasion.

LEISURE ARTS, INC.
Maumelle, Arkansas

Basic Ripple

■■□□ **EASY**

Finished Size: Approximately 49" x 65" (124.5 cm x 165 cm)

SHOPPING LIST

Yarn (Medium Weight)

Caron® Simply Soft®

[5 ounces, 250 yards
(141.7 grams, 228 meters) per skein]:

☐ Color A, #9508 Charcoal Heather -
5 skeins

☐ Color B, #9509 Grey Heather -
5 skeins

[6 ounces, 315 yards
(170.1 grams, 288 meters) per skein]:

☐ Color C, #9773 Neon Yellow -
1 skein

Crochet Hook

☐ Size H (5 mm)
or size needed for gauge

GAUGE INFORMATION

In pattern, one repeat (one ch-1 sp
and 12 dc) = 3¼" (8.25 cm);
9 rows = 5" (12.75 cm)
Gauge Swatch: 6¾"w x 5"h
(17.25 cm x 12.75 cm)
With Color A, ch 30.
Work same as afghan Rows 1-9; at
end of Row 9, do **not** change colors,
finish off: 26 dc and 2 ch-1 sps.

INSTRUCTIONS

With Color A, ch 199.

Row 1: Dc in fifth ch from hook and
in next 4 chs **(4 skipped chs count
as first dc plus 1 skipped ch)**,
(dc, ch 1, dc) in next ch, dc in next
5 chs, ★ skip next 2 chs, dc in next
5 chs, (dc, ch 1, dc) in next ch, dc in
next 5 chs; repeat from ★ across to
last 2 chs, skip next ch, dc in last ch:
182 dc and 15 ch-1 sps.

Rows 2 and 3: Ch 3 **(counts as first
dc)**, turn; skip next dc, dc in next
5 dc, (dc, ch 1, dc) in next ch-1 sp, dc
in next 5 dc, ★ skip next 2 dc, dc in
next 5 dc, (dc, ch 1, dc) in next
ch-1 sp, dc in next 5 dc; repeat from
★ across to last 2 dc, skip next dc, dc
in last dc.

Row 4: Repeat Row 2 changing to
Color C in last dc *(Fig. 8b, page 47)*;
cut Color A.

Row 5: Repeat Row 2 changing to
Color A in last dc; cut Color C.

Rows 6-8: Repeat Row 2, 3 times.

Row 9: Repeat Row 2 changing to
Color B in last dc; cut Color A.

Stripe Sequence: ★ 4 Rows Color B, 1 row Color C, 4 rows Color B, 4 rows Color A, 1 row Color C, 4 rows Color A; repeat from ★ for sequence.

Working in Stripe Sequence, repeat Row 2 for pattern until afghan measures approximately 65" (165 cm) from lowest point on ripple to highest point on last row, ending by working a complete Stripe Sequence.

Finish off.

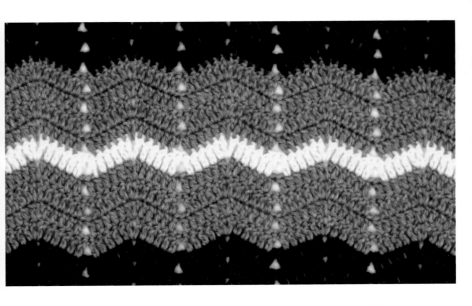

Zeal

 **EASY**

Finished Size: Approximately 47" x 67½" (119.5 cm x 171.5 cm)

SHOPPING LIST

Yarn (Medium Weight)

Caron® Simply Soft®

[6 ounces, 315 yards
(170.1 grams, 288 meters) per skein]:

- ☐ Color A, #9711 Dark Country Blue -
  4 skeins
- ☐ Color B, #0015 Strawberry -
  3 skeins
- ☐ Color C, #9701 White - 3 skeins

Crochet Hook

- ☐ Size I (5.5 mm)
  or size needed for gauge

GAUGE INFORMATION

In pattern,

    one repeat (13 sts) = 2¹/₂" (6.25 cm);

    8 rows = 3" (7.5 cm)

Gauge Swatch: 5"w x 3"h

    (12.75 cm x 7.5 cm)

With Color A, ch 24.

Work same as Body Rows 1-8: 26 sc.

Each row is worked across length of Afghan.

INSTRUCTIONS
BODY

With Color A, ch 324.

Row 1: Sc in second ch from hook and in next 4 chs, 3 sc in next ch, sc in next 5 chs, ★ skip next ch, sc in next 5 chs, 3 sc in next ch, sc in next 5 chs; repeat from ★ across: 351 sc.

Row 2 (Right side)**:** Ch 1, turn; sc in first sc, working in Front Loops Only *(Fig. 4, page 46)*, skip next sc, sc in next 4 sc, 3 sc in next sc, ★ sc in next 5 sc, skip next 2 sc, sc in next 5 sc, 3 sc in next sc; repeat from ★ across to last 6 sc, sc in next 4 sc, skip next sc, sc in **both** loops of last sc.

Note: Loop a short piece of yarn around any stitch to mark Row 2 as **right** side.

Rows 3-12: Repeat Row 2, 10 times changing to Color B in last sc made on Row 12 *(Fig. 8a, page 47)*, cut Color A.

Rows 13-120: Repeat Row 2 for pattern working in the following stripe sequence and changing colors in the same manner: 12 Rows **each** of ★ Color B, Color C, Color A; repeat from ★ 2 times **more** for sequence; at end of Row 120, do **not** change colors **or** finish off.

TRIM

FIRST SIDE

Ch 2, turn; skip first 2 sc, (slip st in next sc, ch 2, skip next sc) twice, (slip st, ch 2, slip st) in next sc, ★ ch 2, (skip next sc, slip st in next sc, ch 2) twice, skip next sc, slip st in next 2 sc, ch 2, skip next sc, (slip st in next sc, ch 2, skip next sc) twice, (slip st, ch 2, slip st) in next sc; repeat from ★ across to last 6 sc, (ch 2, skip next sc, slip st in next sc) 3 times; finish off.

SECOND SIDE

With **wrong** side facing and working in free loops of beginning ch *(Fig. 7, page 47)*, join Color A with slip st in first ch; slip st in next ch, ch 2, skip next ch, slip st in next ch, (ch 1, skip next ch, slip st in next ch) twice, ★ ch 2, skip next ch, slip st in next ch, ch 2, skip next ch, (slip st, ch 2, slip st) in next sp, (ch 2, skip next ch, slip st in next ch) twice, (ch 1, skip next ch, slip st in next ch) twice; repeat from ★ across to last 3 chs, ch 2, skip next ch, slip st in last 2 chs; finish off.

Design by Anne Halliday.

Dynamic Chevron

 **EASY**

Finished Size: Approximately 48¹/₂" x 66¹/₂" (123 cm x 169 cm)

SHOPPING LIST

Yarn (Medium Weight)

Caron® Simply Soft®

[6 ounces, 315 yards
(170.1 grams, 288 meters) per skein]:

- ☐ Color A, #9754 Persimmon - 3 skeins
- ☐ Color B, #0016 Melon - 3 skeins
- ☐ Color C, #9737 Lt Country Peach -
  3 skeins
- ☐ Color D, #9701 White - 3 skeins

Crochet Hook

- ☐ Size I (5.5 mm)
  or size needed for gauge

GAUGE INFORMATION

In pattern,

    one repeat = 6" (15.25 cm);

    6 rows = 4" (10 cm)

Gauge Swatch: 12"w x 4"h

    (30.5 cm x 10 cm)

With Color A, ch 66.

Work same as Body Rows 1-6:

2 6-dc groups and 12 3-dc groups.

Finish off.

—— STITCH GUIDE ——

SINGLE CROCHET 2 TOGETHER

(abbreviated sc2tog)

(uses 2 sps)

Pull up a loop in sp **before** each of next 2 sts, YO and draw through all 3 loops on hook.

DOUBLE CROCHET 2 TOGETHER

(abbreviated dc2tog)

(uses 2 sps)

YO, insert hook in sp **before** next st, YO and pull up a loop, YO and draw through 2 loops on hook (2 loops on hook), YO, skip next st, insert hook in sp **before** next dc, YO and pull up a loop, YO and draw through 2 loops on hook, YO and draw through all 3 loops on hook.

ENDING DECREASE

YO, insert hook in same sp as last dc, YO and pull up a loop, YO and draw through 2 loops on hook (2 loops on hook), YO, skip next 2 dc, insert hook in last dc, YO and pull up a loop, YO and draw through 2 loops on hook, YO and draw through all 3 loops on hook (**counts as last dc**).

INSTRUCTIONS
BODY

With Color A, ch 282; place marker in second ch from hook for Edging placement.

Row 1 (Right side)**:** 3 Dc in fourth ch from hook, (skip next 3 chs, 3 dc in next ch) twice, skip next 3 chs, 6 dc in next ch, ★ (skip next 3 chs, 3 dc in next ch) 3 times, (YO, skip next 3 chs, insert hook in next ch, YO and pull up a loop, YO and draw through 2 loops on hook) twice, YO and draw through all 3 loops on hook, (skip next 3 chs, 3 dc in next ch) 3 times, skip next 3 chs, 6 dc in next ch; repeat from ★ across to last 14 chs, (skip next 3 chs, 3 dc in next ch) twice, skip next 3 chs, 2 dc in next ch, YO, insert hook in same ch, YO and pull up a loop, YO and draw through 2 loops on hook, YO, skip next ch, insert hook in last ch, YO and pull up a loop, YO and draw through 2 loops on hook, YO and draw through all 3 loops on hook **(counts as last dc)**: 8 6-dc groups and 48 3-dc groups.

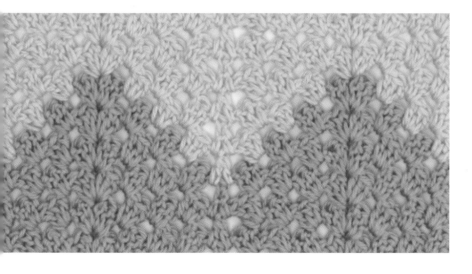

13

Note: Loop a short piece of yarn around any stitch to mark Row 1 as **right** side.

Row 2: Ch 2, turn; skip first 3-dc group, 3 dc in sp **before** next 3-dc group *(Fig. 6, page 46)*, (skip next 3-dc group, 3 dc in sp before next 3-dc group) twice, skip next 3 dc, 6 dc in sp before next dc (center of 6-dc group), ★ skip next 3 dc, (3 dc in sp before next 3-dc group, skip next 3-dc group) 3 times, dc2tog, (skip next 3-dc group, 3 dc in sp before next 3-dc group) 3 times, skip next 3 dc, 6 dc in sp before next dc (center of 6-dc group); repeat from ★ across to last 12 dc, skip next 3 dc, (3 dc in sp before next 3-dc group, skip next 3-dc group) twice, 2 dc in sp before last 3-dc group, work ending decrease.

Repeat Row 2, working a total of 24 rows of **each** color in the following stripe sequence *(Fig. 8b, page 47)*: Color A, Color B, Color C, and Color D; at end of last row, do **not** change colors and do **not** finish off.

EDGING

Ch 1, turn; (sc, ch 2) twice in first dc, skip next 2 dc, (sc in sp before next group, ch 2, skip next dc, sc in next dc, ch 2, skip next dc) 3 times, (sc, ch 2) twice in sp before next dc, ★ skip next dc, sc in next dc, ch 2, (skip next dc, sc in sp before next group, ch 2, skip next dc, sc in next dc, ch 2) 3 times, skip next dc, sc2tog, ch 2, skip next dc, sc in next dc, ch 2, (skip next dc, sc in sp before next group, ch 2, skip next dc, sc in next dc, ch 2) 3 times, skip next dc, (sc, ch 2) twice in sp before next dc; repeat from ★

6 times **more**, (skip next dc, sc in next dc, ch 2, skip next dc, sc in sp before next group, ch 2) 3 times, skip next 2 dc, (sc, ch 2) twice in last dc; **working in end of rows**, sc in first row, ch 2, (sc in next row, ch 2) across; **working in sps and in free loops of beginning ch** *(Fig. 7, page 47)*, (sc, ch 2) twice in first ch, sc in ch at base of next group, ch 2, (sc in next sp, ch 2, sc in ch at base of next group, ch 2) twice, pull up a loop in each of next 2 sps, YO and draw through all 3 loops on hook, ch 2, (sc in ch at base of next group, ch 2, sc in next sp, ch 2) 3 times, † (sc, ch 2) twice in next sp, (sc in next sp, ch 2, sc in ch at base of next group, ch 2) 3 times, pull up a loop in each of next 2 sps, YO and draw through all 3 loops on hook, ch 2, (sc in ch at base of next group, ch 2, sc in next sp, ch 2) 3 times †; repeat from † to † across to marked ch, (sc, ch 2) twice in marked ch, remove marker; **working in end of rows**, sc in same row, ch 2, (sc in next row, ch 2) across; join with slip st to first sc, finish off.

Design by Tammy Kreimeyer.

Radiance

 **EASY**

Finished Size: Approximately 49¹/₂" x 69¹/₂" (125.5 cm x 176.5 cm)

SHOPPING LIST

Yarn (Medium Weight)

Caron® Simply Soft®

[6 ounces, 315 yards
(170.1 grams, 288 meters) per skein]:

☐ Main Color, #9727 Black - 5 skeins

☐ Color A, #9604 Watermelon -
2 skeins

☐ Color B, #9607 Limelight - 2 skeins

☐ Color C, #9605 Mango - 2 skeins

Crochet Hook

☐ Size I (5.5 mm)

or size needed for gauge

GAUGE INFORMATION

In pattern,

    one repeat (24 sts) = 5½" (14 cm);

    6 rows = 4½" (11.5 cm)

Gauge Swatch: 11"w x 4½"h

    (28 cm x 11.5 cm)

With Main Color, ch 50.

Work same as afghan Rows 1-6:

49 dc.

──── STITCH GUIDE ────

DOUBLE CROCHET 2 TOGETHER

(abbreviated dc2tog)

(uses next 2 sts)

★ YO, insert hook in **next** st, YO and pull up a loop, YO and draw through 2 loops on hook; repeat from ★ once **more**, YO and draw through all 3 loops on hook (**counts as one dc**).

DOUBLE CROCHET 3 TOGETHER

(abbreviated dc3tog)

(uses next 3 sts)

★ YO, insert hook in **next** st, YO and pull up a loop, YO and draw through 2 loops on hook; repeat from ★ 2 times **more**, YO and draw through all 4 loops on hook (**counts as one dc**).

DOUBLE CROCHET 5 TOGETHER

(abbreviated dc5tog)

(uses next 5 sts)

★ YO, insert hook in **next** st, YO and pull up a loop, YO and draw through 2 loops on hook; repeat from ★ 4 times **more**, YO and draw through all 6 loops on hook (**counts as one dc**).

LONG FRONT POST TREBLE CROCHET (abbreviated LFPtr)

Working in **front** of previous row, YO twice, insert hook from **front** to **back** around post of dc on row **below** next dc *(Fig. A)*, YO and pull up a long loop (4 loops on hook), (YO and draw through 2 loops on hook) 3 times. Skip dc behind LFPtr.

Fig. A

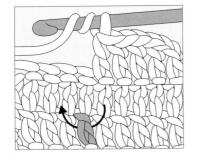

INSTRUCTIONS

With Main Color, ch 218.

Row 1 (Right side)**:** Dc2tog beginning in third ch from hook, dc in next 9 chs, 5 dc in next ch, dc in next 9 chs, ★ dc5tog, dc in next 9 chs, 5 dc in next ch, dc in next 9 chs; repeat from ★ across to last 3 chs, dc3tog: 217 dc.

Note: Loop a short piece of yarn around any stitch to mark Row 1 as **right** side.

Row 2: Ch 2, turn; skip first st, dc2tog, dc in next 9 dc, 5 dc in next dc, dc in next 9 dc, ★ dc5tog, dc in next 9 dc, 5 dc in next dc, dc in next 9 dc; repeat from ★ across to last 3 dc, dc3tog; finish off.

Row 3: With **right** side facing, join Color A with slip st in first st; ch 2, skip joining st, dc2tog, dc in next 5 dc, work LFPtr, dc in next 3 dc, 5 dc in next dc, dc in next 3 dc, work LFPtr, dc in next 5 dc, ★ dc5tog, dc in next 5 dc, work LFPtr, dc in next 3 dc, 5 dc in next dc, dc in next 3 dc, work LFPtr, dc in next 5 dc; repeat from ★ across to last 3 dc, dc3tog.

Row 4: Ch 2, turn; skip first st, dc2tog, dc in next 9 sts, 5 dc in next dc, dc in next 9 sts, ★ dc5tog, dc in next 9 sts, 5 dc in next dc, dc in next 9 sts; repeat from ★ across to last 3 dc, dc3tog; finish off.

Rows 5-90: Repeat Rows 3 and 4 for pattern working in the following stripe sequence: 2 Rows **each** of Main Color, ★ Color B, Main Color, Color C, Main Color, Color A, Main Color; repeat from ★ 6 times **more** for sequence.

Design by Darla Sims.

Lacy Chevron

 **INTERMEDIATE**

Finished Size: Approximately 49" x 65" (124.5 cm x 165 cm)

Shown on page 23.

SHOPPING LIST

Yarn (Medium Weight) 🧶 **4** MEDIUM

Caron® Simply Soft®

[6 ounces, 315 yards

(170.1 grams, 288 meters) per skein]:

- ☐ Main Color, #9701 White - 4 skeins
- ☐ Color A, #9776 Lemonade - 2 skeins
- ☐ Color B, #9608 Blue Mint - 2 skeins
- ☐ Color C, #9729 Red - 2 skeins

Crochet Hook

- ☐ Size I (5.5 mm)

     or size needed for gauge

GAUGE INFORMATION

In pattern,

    one repeat = 5" (12.75 cm);

    6 rows = 3" (7.5 cm)

Gauge Swatch: 7³/₄"w x 3"h

    (19.75 cm x 7.5 cm)

With Main Color, ch 34.

Work same as Body Rows 1-6: 28 sts and 7 sps.

INSTRUCTIONS
BODY

With Main Color, ch 210.

Row 1 (Right side)**:** Sc in second ch from hook and in next 4 chs, (sc, ch 2, sc) in next ch, ★ sc in next 4 chs, skip next 2 chs, (dc in next ch, ch 1, skip next ch) twice, (dc, ch 2, dc) in next ch, (ch 1, skip next ch, dc in next ch) twice, skip next 2 chs, sc in next 4 chs, (sc, ch 2, sc) in next ch; repeat from ★ across to last 5 chs, sc in last 5 chs; finish off: 156 sts and 55 sps.

Note: Loop a short piece of yarn around any stitch to mark Row 1 as **right** side.

Row 2: With **wrong** side facing, join Color A with dc in first sc *(Fig. 3, page 45)*; skip next sc, dc in next 4 sc, (dc, ch 2, dc) in next ch-2 sp, dc in next 4 sc, ★ skip next 2 sts, (sc in next ch-1 sp, ch 1) twice, (sc, ch 2, sc) in next ch-2 sp, (ch 1, sc in next ch-1 sp) twice, skip next 2 sts, dc in next 4 sc, (dc, ch 2, dc) in next ch-2 sp, dc in next 4 sc; repeat from ★ across to last 2 sc, skip next sc, dc in last sc; finish off.

Row 3: With **right** side facing, join Main Color with sc in first dc *(Figs. 2a & b, page 45)*; skip next dc, sc in next 4 dc, (sc, ch 2, sc) in next ch-2 sp, sc in next 4 dc, ★ skip next 2 sts, (dc in next ch-1 sp, ch 1) twice, (dc, ch 2, dc) in next ch-2 sp, (ch 1, dc in next ch-1 sp) twice, skip next 2 sts, sc in next 4 dc, (sc, ch 2, sc) in next ch-2 sp, sc in next 4 dc; repeat from ★ across to last 2 dc, skip next dc, sc in last dc; finish off.

Row 4: With Color B, repeat Row 2.

Row 5: Repeat Row 3.

Row 6: With Color C, repeat Row 2.

Row 7: Repeat Row 3.

Repeat Rows 2-7 for pattern until Body measures approximately 64" (162.5 cm) from lowest point on ripple to highest point on last row, ending by working Row 3 (one row after a Color A row), do **not** finish off.

EDGING

Rnd 1: Ch 1, do **not** turn; **working in end of rows**, slip st in first row, ch 3, (skip next row, slip st in next row, ch 3) across; **working in sps and in free loops of beginning ch** *(Fig. 7, page 47)*, slip st in first ch, place marker around last ch-3 made to mark corner, (ch 2, skip next ch, slip st in next ch) twice, (skip next ch, slip st in next ch, ch 2) twice, ★ skip next ch, (slip st, ch 3, slip st) in next sp, ch 2, slip st in next sp, ch 2, slip st in next 2 sps, ch 2, slip st in next sp, ch 2, (slip st, ch 3, slip st) in next sp, (ch 2, skip next ch, slip st in next ch) twice, (skip next ch, slip st in next ch, ch 2) twice; repeat from ★ 8 times **more**, skip next ch, slip st in next ch, ch 3; **working in end of rows**, slip st in first row, place marker around last ch-3 made to mark corner, ch 3, (skip next row, slip st in next row, ch 3) across; **working across last row**, slip st in first sc, place marker around last ch-3 made to mark corner, ch 2, skip next sc, (slip st in next sc, ch 2, skip next sc) twice, (slip st, ch 3, slip st) in next ch-2 sp, (ch 2, skip next sc, slip st in next sc) twice, † skip next 2 sts, (slip st in next ch-1 sp, ch 2) twice, (slip st, ch 3, slip st) in next ch-2 sp, (ch 2, slip st in next ch-1 sp) twice, skip next 2 sts, (slip st in next sc, ch 2, skip next sc) twice, (slip st, ch 3, slip st) in next ch-2 sp, (ch 2, skip next sc, slip st in next sc) twice †; repeat from † to † across to last 2 sc, skip last 2 sc, dc in first slip st to form last ch-3 sp.

Rnd 2: (Slip st, ch 3, dc) in last ch-3 sp made and in each ch-3 sp across to next marked corner, remove marker, ★ (slip st, ch 3, slip st) in next ch-3 sp, (ch 2, slip st in next ch-2 sp) twice, skip next slip st, slip st in next slip st and in next ch-2 sp, ch 2, slip st in next ch-2 sp, ch 2; repeat from ★ across to next marked corner, remove marker, **[**(slip st, ch 3) twice, dc**]** in corner ch-3 sp, (slip st, ch 3, dc) in each ch-3 sp across and in next marked corner, remove marker, (slip st in next ch-2 sp, ch 2) 3 times, (slip st, ch 3, slip st) in next ch-3 sp, † (ch 2, slip st in next ch-2 sp) twice, skip next slip st, slip st in next slip st and in next ch-2 sp, ch 2, slip st in next ch-2 sp, ch 2, (slip st, ch 3, slip st) in next ch-3 sp †; repeat from † to † across to last 2 ch-2 sps, ch 2, (slip st in next ch-2 sp, ch 2) twice; join with slip st to first slip st, finish off.

Design by Anne Halliday.

Snowcapped Ripple

 **EASY**

Finished Size: Approximately 48" x 65" (122 cm x 165 cm)

Shown on page 29.

SHOPPING LIST

Yarn (Medium Weight) 🔢 4

Caron® Simply Soft®

[5 ounces, 250 yards
(141.7 grams, 228 meters) per skein]:

☐ Color A, #9509 Grey Heather -
   5 skeins

[6 ounces, 315 yards
(170.1 grams, 288 meters) per skein]:

☐ Color B, #9727 Black - 3 skeins
☐ Color C, #9701 White - 3 skeins

Crochet Hook

☐ Size I (5.5 mm)
   or size needed for gauge

GAUGE INFORMATION

In pattern,

one repeat (14 sts) = 4" (10 cm);

6 rows = 3½" (9 cm)

Gauge Swatch: 8"w x 3½"h

(20.25 cm x 9 cm)

With Color A, ch 32.

Work same as afghan Rows 1-6; at end of Row 6, do **not** change colors, finish off: 29 dc.

—— STITCH GUIDE ——

SINGLE CROCHET 3 TOGETHER

(abbreviated sc3tog)

(uses next 3 dc)

Pull up a loop in each of next 3 dc, YO and draw through all 4 loops on hook **(counts as one sc)**.

DOUBLE CROCHET 3 TOGETHER

(abbreviated dc3tog)

(uses next 3 sts)

★ YO, insert hook in next st, YO and pull up a loop, YO and draw through 2 loops on hook; repeat from ★ 2 times **more**, YO and draw through all 4 loops on hook **(counts as one dc)**.

CLUSTER (uses one dc)

★ YO, insert hook in dc indicated, YO and pull up a loop, YO and draw through 2 loops on hook; repeat from ★ 3 times **more**, YO and draw through all 5 loops on hook. Push Cluster to **right** side.

INSTRUCTIONS

With Color A, ch 172.

Row 1 (Wrong side)**:** Working in back ridges of beginning ch *(Fig. 1, page 43)*, dc in fourth ch from hook **(3 skipped chs count as first dc)** and in next 5 chs, dc3tog, dc in next 5 chs, ★ 3 dc in next ch, dc in next 5 chs, dc3tog, dc in next 5 chs; repeat from ★ across to last ch, 2 dc in last ch: 169 dc.

Note: Loop a short piece of yarn around **back** of any stitch on Row 1 to mark **right** side.

Row 2: Ch 3 **(counts as first dc, now and throughout)**, turn; dc in same st and in next 5 dc, dc3tog, dc in next 5 dc, ★ 3 dc in next dc, dc in next 5 dc, dc3tog, dc in next 5 dc; repeat from ★ across to last dc, 2 dc in last dc.

Row 3: Ch 3, turn; dc in same st and in next 5 sts, dc3tog, dc in next 5 sts, ★ 3 dc in next st, dc in next 5 sts, dc3tog, dc in next 5 sts; repeat from ★ across to last st, 2 dc in last st changing to Color B in last dc made *(Fig. 8b, page 47)*; cut previous color.

Row 4: Repeat Row 3 changing to Color C in last dc made.

Row 5: Ch 1, turn; 2 sc in first dc, work Cluster in next dc, (sc in next dc, work Cluster in next dc) twice, sc3tog, work Cluster in next dc, (sc in next dc, work Cluster in next dc) twice, ★ 3 sc in next dc, work Cluster in next dc, (sc in next dc, work Cluster in next dc) twice, sc3tog, work Cluster in next dc, (sc in next dc, work Cluster in next dc) twice; repeat from ★ across to last dc, 2 sc in last dc changing to Color B in last sc made: 97 sc and 72 Clusters.

Row 6: Repeat Row 3 changing to Color A in last dc made: 169 dc.

Rows 7 and 8: Ch 3, turn; dc in same st and in next 5 dc, dc3tog, dc in next 5 dc, ★ 3 dc in next dc, dc in next 5 dc, dc3tog, dc in next 5 dc; repeat from ★ across to last dc, 2 dc in last dc.

Repeat Rows 3-8 for pattern until afghan measures approximately 65" (165 cm) from beginning point, ending by working Row 3; at end of last row, do **not** change colors, finish off.

Design by Melissa Leapman.

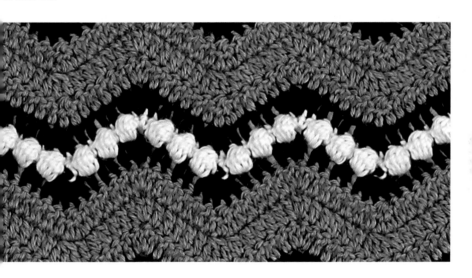

Fresh Flowers

 **INTERMEDIATE**

Finished Size: Approximately 46" x 64" (117 cm x 162.5 cm)

SHOPPING LIST

Yarn (Medium Weight)

Caron® Simply Soft®

[6 ounces, 315 yards

(170.1 grams, 288 meters) per skein]:

- ☐ Main Color, #9701 White - 6 skeins
- ☐ Contrasting Color, #0012 Passion - 2 skeins

Crochet Hook

- ☐ Size G (4 mm)

  or size needed for gauge

GAUGE INFORMATION

In pattern, one point to

point repeat = 7½" (19 cm);

Rows 1-11 = 6½" (16.5 cm)

Gauge Swatch: 14¼"w x 4¾"h

(36.25 cm x 12 cm)

With Main Color, ch 63.

Work same as Body for 7 rows:

63 sts.

——— STITCH GUIDE ———

3-DC CLUSTER (uses one st)

★ YO, insert hook in st indicated, YO and pull up a loop, YO and draw through 2 loops on hook; repeat from ★ 2 times **more**, YO and draw through all 4 loops on hook.

5-DC CLUSTER (uses one st)

★ YO, insert hook in st indicated, YO and pull up a loop, YO and draw through 2 loops on hook; repeat from ★ 4 times **more**, YO and draw through all 6 loops on hook.

SINGLE CROCHET 2 TOGETHER

(abbreviated sc2tog)

(uses next 2 dc)

Pull up a loop in each of next 2 dc, YO and draw through all 3 loops on hook (**counts as one sc**).

DOUBLE CROCHET 2 TOGETHER

(abbreviated dc2tog)

(uses next 2 sts)

★ YO, insert hook in **next** st, YO and pull up a loop, YO and draw through 2 loops on hook; repeat from ★ once **more**, YO and draw through all 3 loops on hook (**counts as one dc**).

INSTRUCTIONS
BODY

With Main Color, ch 191.

Row 1 (Right side)**:** Dc in fourth ch from hook (**3 skipped chs count as first dc**) and in next 12 chs, 3 dc in next ch, dc in next 14 chs, ★ skip next ch, work 5-dc Cluster in next ch, skip next ch, dc in next 14 chs, 3 dc in next ch, dc in next 14 chs; repeat from ★ across; finish off: 186 dc and 5 5-dc Clusters.

Note: Loop a short piece of yarn around any stitch to mark Row 1 as **right** side.

Work in Back Loops Only throughout *(Fig. 4, page 46)* unless otherwise specified.

Row 2: With **right** side facing, join Main Color with dc in first dc *(Fig. 3, page 45)*; dc2tog, dc in next 6 dc, ch 5, skip next 2 dc, dc in next 4 dc, 3 dc in next dc, dc in next 4 dc, ch 5, ★ skip next 2 dc, dc in next 8 dc, skip next dc, work 5-dc Cluster in **both** loops of next 5-dc Cluster, skip next dc, dc in next 8 dc, ch 5, skip next 2 dc, dc in next 4 dc, 3 dc in next dc, dc in next 4 dc, ch 5; repeat from ★ 4 times **more**, skip next 2 dc, dc in next 6 dc, dc2tog, dc in last dc; finish off: 167 sts and 12 ch-5 sps.

Row 3: With **right** side facing, join Main Color with dc in first dc; dc2tog, dc in next 3 dc, ★ † ch 3, sc in next ch-5 sp, ch 3, skip next 2 dc, dc in next 3 dc, 3 dc in next dc, dc in next 3 dc, ch 3, sc in next ch-5 sp, ch 3 †, skip next 2 dc, dc in next 5 dc, skip next dc, work 5-dc Cluster in **both** loops of next 5-dc Cluster, skip next dc, dc in next 5 dc; repeat from ★ 4 times **more**, then repeat from † to † once, skip next 2 dc, dc in next 3 dc, dc2tog, dc in last dc; finish off: 131 sts and 24 ch-3 sps.

Row 4: With **right** side facing, join Main Color with dc in first dc; dc2tog, ★ † ch 5, sc in next ch-3 sp, work 3-dc Cluster in **both** loops of next sc, sc in next ch-3 sp, ch 5, skip next 2 dc, dc in next 2 dc, 3 dc in next dc, dc in next 2 dc, ch 5, sc in next ch-3 sp, work 3-dc Cluster in **both** loops of next sc, sc in next ch-3 sp, ch 5 †, skip next 2 dc, dc in next 2 dc, skip next dc, work 5-dc Cluster in **both** loops of next 5-dc Cluster, skip next dc, dc in next 2 dc; repeat from ★ 4 times **more**, then repeat from † to † once, skip next 2 dc, dc2tog, dc in last dc; finish off: 107 sts and 24 ch-5 sps.

Row 5: With **right** side facing, join Main Color with slip st in first dc; ch 2, ★ † dc in next dc and in next 2 chs, ch 3, skip next sc, sc in **both** loops of next 3-dc Cluster, ch 3, skip next 3 chs, dc in next 2 chs and in next 3 dc, 3 dc in next dc, dc in next 3 dc and in next 2 chs, ch 3, skip next sc, sc in **both** loops of next 3-dc Cluster, ch 3 †, skip next 3 chs, dc in next 2 chs and in next dc, skip next dc, work 5-dc Cluster in **both** loops of next 5-dc Cluster, skip next dc; repeat from ★ 4 times **more**, then repeat from † to † once, skip next 3 chs, dc in next 2 chs, dc2tog; finish off: 131 sts and 24 ch-3 sps.

Row 6: With **right** side facing, join Main Color with dc in first dc; dc2tog, dc in next 2 chs, ★ † ch 2, skip next sc and next ch, dc in next 2 chs and in next 6 dc, 3 dc in next dc, dc in next 6 dc and in next 2 chs, ch 2, skip next sc and next ch †, dc in next 2 chs and next 2 dc, skip next dc, work 5-dc Cluster in **both** loops of next 5-dc Cluster, skip next dc, dc in next 2 dc and in next 2 chs; repeat from ★ 4 times **more**, then repeat from † to † once, dc in next 2 chs, dc2tog, dc in last dc; finish off: 167 sts and 12 ch-2 sps.

Row 7: With **right** side facing, join Main Color with dc in first dc; dc2tog, dc in next dc and in next 2 chs, ★ † dc in next 9 dc, 3 dc in next dc, dc in next 9 dc and in next 2 chs †, dc in next 3 dc, skip next dc, work 5-dc Cluster in **both** loops of next 5-dc Cluster, skip next dc, dc in next 3 dc and in next 2 chs; repeat from ★ 4 times **more**, then repeat from † to † once, dc in next dc, dc2tog, dc in last dc; finish off: 191 sts.

Row 8: With **right** side facing, join Contrasting Color with dc in first dc; dc2tog, dc in next 12 dc, 3 dc in next dc, ★ dc in next 14 dc, skip next 3 sts, dc in next 14 dc, 3 dc in next dc; repeat from ★ 4 times **more**, dc in next 12 dc, dc2tog, dc in last dc; finish off: 186 dc.

Row 9: With **right** side facing, join Main Color with sc in first dc *(Figs. 2a & b, page 45)*; sc2tog, sc in next 12 dc, 3 sc in next dc, ★ sc in next 14 dc, working in **front** of sts on previous row *(Fig. 5, page 46)*, work 5-dc Cluster in **both** loops of skipped 5-dc Cluster one row **below**, skip next 2 sts on previous row from last sc made, sc in next 14 dc, 3 sc in next dc; repeat from ★ 4 times **more**, sc in next 12 dc, sc2tog, sc in last dc; finish off: 191 sts.

Row 10: With **right** side facing, join Contrasting Color with dc in first sc; dc2tog, dc in next 12 sc, 3 dc in next sc, ★ dc in next 14 sc, skip next 3 sts, dc in next 14 sc, 3 dc in next sc; repeat from ★ 4 times **more**, dc in next 12 sc, dc2tog, dc in last sc; finish off: 186 dc.

Row 11: Repeat Row 9: 191 sts.

Row 12: With **right** side facing, join Main Color with dc in first sc; dc2tog, dc in next 12 sc, 3 dc in next sc, ★ dc in next 14 sc, skip next sc, work 5-dc Cluster in **both** loops of next 5-dc Cluster, skip next sc, dc in next 14 sc, 3 dc in next sc; repeat from ★ 4 times **more**, dc in next 12 dc, dc2tog, dc in last dc; finish off.

Rows 13-106: Repeat Rows 2-12, 8 times; then repeat Rows 2-7 once **more**; at end of Row 106, do **not** finish off.

EDGING

Ch 1; with **right** side facing, (sc, ch 3, work 3-dc Cluster) in top of last dc made on Row 106; **working in end of rows**, (sc, ch 3, work 3-dc Cluster) in top of next 7 rows, skip next row, (sc, ch 3, work 3-dc Cluster) in top of next row, skip next row, [(sc, ch 3, work 3-dc Cluster) in top of next 8 rows, skip next row, (sc, ch 3, work 3-dc Cluster) in top of next row, skip next row] 8 times, (sc, ch 3, work 3-dc Cluster) in top of next 7 rows; **working in free loops of beginning ch** (*Fig. 7, page 47*), (sc, ch 3, work 3-dc Cluster) twice in first ch, skip next ch, † [(sc, ch 3, work 3-dc Cluster) in next ch, skip next 2 chs] 9 times, (sc, ch 3, work 3-dc Cluster) in next 2 ch-1 sps, skip next 2 chs †; repeat from † to † 4 times **more**, (sc, ch 3, work 3-dc Cluster) in next ch, [skip next 2 chs, (sc, ch 3, work 3-dc Cluster) in next ch] 8 times, (sc, ch 3, work 3-dc Cluster) twice in next ch; **working in end of rows**, (sc, ch 3, work 3-dc Cluster) in top of first 7 rows, [skip next row, (sc, ch 3, work 3-dc Cluster) in top of next row, skip next row, (sc, ch 3, work 3-dc Cluster) in top of next 8 rows] across; **working in both loops of sts across Row 106**, [skip next dc, (sc, ch 3, work 3-dc Cluster) in next dc, skip next 2 dc, (sc, ch 3, work 3-dc Cluster) in next dc] 3 times, ★ [skip next 2 dc, (sc, ch 3, work 3-dc Cluster) in next dc, skip next dc, (sc, ch 3, work 3-dc Cluster) in next dc] twice, [skip next 2 dc, (sc, ch 3, work 3-dc Cluster) in next st] 4 times, [skip next dc, (sc, ch 3, work 3-dc Cluster) in next dc, skip next 2 dc, (sc, ch 3, work 3-dc Cluster) in next dc] twice; repeat from ★ 4 times **more**, skip next 2 dc, (sc, ch 3, work 3-dc Cluster) in next dc, skip next dc, [(sc, ch 3, work 3-dc Cluster) in next dc, skip next 2 dc, (sc, ch 3, work 3-dc Cluster) in next dc, skip next dc] twice; join with slip st to first sc, finish off.

Design by Pat Gibbons.

General Instructions

ABBREVIATIONS

ch(s)	chain(s)
cm	centimeters
dc	double crochet(s)
dc2tog	double crochet 2 together
dc3tog	double crochet 3 together
dc5tog	double crochet 5 together
LFPtr	Long Front Post treble crochet
mm	millimeters
Rnd(s)	Round(s)
sc	single crochet(s)
sc2tog	single crochet 2 together
sc3tog	single crochet 3 together
sp(s)	space(s)
st(s)	stitch(es)
YO	yarn over

SYMBOLS & TERMS

★ — work instructions following ★ as many **more** times as indicated in addition to the first time.

( ) or [ ] — work enclosed instructions **as many** times as specified by the number immediately following **or** work all enclosed instructions in the stitch or space indicated **or** contains explanatory remarks.

† to † — work all instructions from first † to second † **as many** times as specified.

colon (:) — the number(s) given after a colon at the end of a row or round denote(s) the number of stitches or spaces you should have on that row or round.

CROCHET TERMINOLOGY

UNITED STATES		INTERNATIONAL
slip stitch (slip st)	=	single crochet (sc)
single crochet (sc)	=	double crochet (dc)
half double crochet (hdc)	=	half treble crochet (htr)
double crochet (dc)	=	treble crochet (tr)
treble crochet (tr)	=	double treble crochet (dtr)
double treble crochet (dtr)	=	triple treble crochet (ttr)
triple treble crochet (tr tr)	=	quadruple treble crochet (qtr)
skip	=	miss

◼◻◻◻ **BEGINNER**	Projects for first-time crocheters using basic stitches. Minimal shaping.
◼◼◻◻ **EASY**	Projects using yarn with basic stitches, repetitive stitch patterns, simple color changes, and simple shaping and finishing.
◼◼◼◻ **INTERMEDIATE**	Projects using a variety of techniques, such as basic lace patterns or color patterns, mid-level shaping and finishing.
◼◼◼◼ **EXPERIENCED**	Projects with intricate stitch patterns, techniques and dimension, such as non-repeating patterns, multi-color techniques, fine threads, small hooks, detailed shaping and refined finishing.

CROCHET HOOKS

U.S.	B-1	C-2	D-3	E-4	F-5	G-6	H-8	I-9	J-10	K-10½	L-11	M/N-13	N/P-15	P/Q	Q	S
Metric - mm	2.25	2.75	3.25	3.5	3.75	4	5	5.5	6	6.5	8	9	10	15	16	19

GAUGE

Exact gauge is **essential** for proper size. Before beginning your afghan, make the sample swatch given in the individual instructions in the yarn and hook specified. After completing the swatch, measure it, counting your stitches and rows carefully. If your swatch is larger or smaller than specified, **make another, changing hook size to get the correct gauge.** Keep trying until you find the size hook that will give you the specified gauge.

BACK RIDGES

Work only in loop(s) indicated by arrow *(Fig. 1)*.

Fig. 1

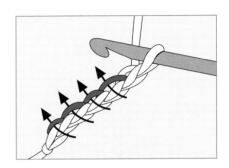

Yarn Weight Symbol & Names	LACE 0	SUPER FINE 1	FINE 2	LIGHT 3	MEDIUM 4	BULKY 5	SUPER BULKY 6
Type of Yarns in Category	Fingering, 10-count crochet thread	Sock, Fingering Baby	Sport, Baby	DK, Light Worsted	Worsted, Afghan, Aran	Chunky, Craft, Rug	Bulky, Roving
Crochet Gauge* Ranges in Single Crochet to 4" (10 cm)	32-42 double crochets**	21-32 sts	16-20 sts	12-17 sts	11-14 sts	8-11 sts	5-9 sts
Advised Hook Size Range	Steel*** 6,7,8 Regular hook B-1	B-1 to E-4	E-4 to 7	7 to I-9	I-9 to K-10½	K-10½ to M/N-13	M/N-13 and larger

*GUIDELINES ONLY: The chart above reflects the most commonly used gauges and hook sizes for specific yarn categories.

** Lace weight yarns are usually crocheted on larger-size hooks to create lacy openwork patterns. Accordingly, a gauge range is difficult to determine. Always follow the gauge stated in your pattern.

*** Steel crochet hooks are sized differently from regular hooks—the higher the number the smaller the hook, which is the reverse of regular hook sizing.

MEASURE YOUR GAUGE AND AFGHAN

Lay your piece on a flat, hard surface. Measure one point-to-point repeat by placing the ruler from the center of one peak increase to the center of the next peak increase.

Measure the height of your gauge swatch by placing the ruler from the bottom of the center stitch of a peak increase to the highest point of the swatch.

Measure the width of your gauge swatch or afghan from straight edge to straight edge. The length of the afghan is measured from the bottom of the lowest valley to the top of the highest peak.

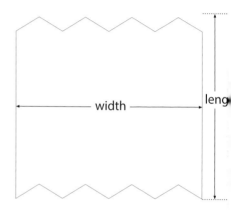

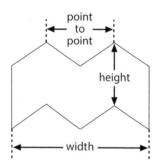

JOINING WITH SC

When instructed to join with sc, begin with a slip knot on hook. Insert hook in stitch or space indicated, YO and pull up a loop, (YO and draw through both loops on hook *(Figs. 2a & b)*.

Fig. 2a

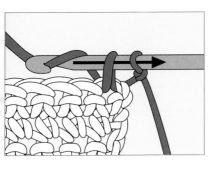

Fig. 2b

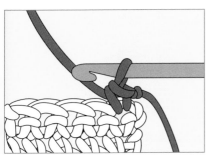

JOINING WITH DC

When instructed to join with dc, begin with a slip knot on hook. YO, holding loop on hook, insert hook in stitch or space indicated, YO and pull up a loop (3 loops on hook), (YO and draw through 2 loops on hook) twice *(Fig. 3)*.

Fig. 3

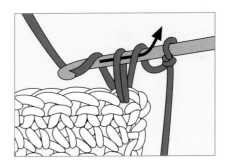

BACK OR FRONT LOOPS ONLY

Work only in loop(s) indicated by arrow *(Fig. 4)*.

Fig. 4

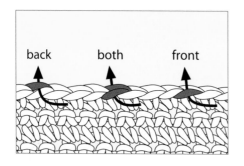

WORKING IN FRONT OF A STITCH

Work in stitch or space indicated, inserting hook in direction of arrow *(Fig. 5)*.

Fig. 5

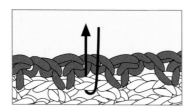

WORKING IN SPACE BEFORE A STITCH

When instructed to work in space before a stitch or in spaces between stitches, insert hook in space indicated by arrow *(Fig. 6)*.

Fig. 6

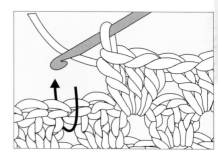

FREE LOOPS OF A CHAIN

When instructed to work in free loops of a chain, work in loop indicated by arrow *(Fig. 7)*.

Fig. 7

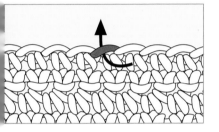

CHANGING COLORS

Work the last stitch to within one step of completion (2 loops on hook), hook new yarn *(Figs. 8a & b)* and draw through both loops on hook.

Cut old yarn and work over both ends.

Fig. 8a

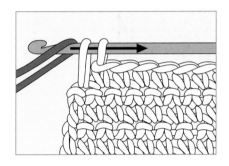

Fig. 8b

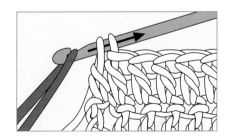

We have made every effort to ensure that these instructions are accurate and complete. We cannot, however, be responsible for human error, typographical mistakes, or variations in individual work.

Production Team: Writer/Technical Editor - Cathy Hardy; Editorial Writer – Susan Frantz Wiles; Senior Graphic Artist – Lora Puls; Graphic Artist - Cailen Cochran; Photo Stylist - Lori Wenger; and Photographer - Jason Masters.

Instructions tested and photo models made by Janet Akins, Marianna Crowder, Lee Ellis, and Raymelle Greening.